SPEECH, MEDIA, AND PROTEST

FOUNDATIONS OF DEMOCRACY

FOUNDATIONS OF DEMOCRACY

SPEECH, MEDIA, AND PROTEST

Robert J. Pauly, Jr.

Series Advisor: Tom Lansford
Professor of Political Science
University of Southern Mississippi, Gulf Coast

MASON CREST

Mason Crest
450 Parkway Drive, Suite D
Broomall, PA 19008
www.masoncrest.com

MTM Publishing, Inc.
435 West 23rd Street, #8C
New York, NY 10011
www.mtmpublishing.com

President: Valerie Tomaselli
Vice President, Book Development: Hilary Poole
Designer: Annemarie Redmond
Copyeditor: Peter Jaskowiak
Editorial Assistant: Andrea St. Aubin

Series ISBN: 978-1-4222-3625-3
Hardback ISBN: 978-1-4222-3633-8
E-Book ISBN: 978-1-4222-8277-9

Library of Congress Cataloging-in-Publication Data
Names: Pauly, Robert J., 1967– author.
Title: Speech, media, and protest / by Robert J. Pauly, Jr.
Description: Broomall, PA: Mason Crest, 2017. | Series: Foundations of
  democracy | Includes index.
Identifiers: LCCN 2016004317 | ISBN 9781422236338 (hardback) | ISBN
  9781422236253 (series) | ISBN 9781422282779 (ebook)
Subjects: LCSH: Freedom of speech—Juvenile literature. | Freedom of the press—Juvenile
  literature. | Freedom of expression—Juvenile literature. | Civil rights—Juvenile literature.
Classification: LCC JC591 .P38 2017 | DDC 323.44/3—dc23
LC record available at https://lccn.loc.gov/2016004317

Printed and bound in the United States of America.

First printing
9 8 7 6 5 4 3 2 1

TABLE OF CONTENTS

Key Icons to Look for:

Words to Understand: These words with their easy-to-understand definitions will increase the reader's understanding of the text, while building vocabulary skills.

Sidebars: This boxed material within the main text allows readers to build knowledge, gain insights, explore possibilities, and broaden their perspectives by weaving together additional information to provide realistic and holistic perspectives.

Research Projects: Readers are pointed toward areas of further inquiry connected to each chapter. Suggestions are provided for projects that encourage deeper research and analysis.

Text-Dependent Questions: These questions send the reader back to the text for more careful attention to the evidence presented there.

Series Glossary of Key Terms: This back-of-the-book glossary contains terminology used throughout the series. Words found here increase the reader's ability to read and comprehend higher-level books and articles in this field.

Iraqi women at a political rally in 2010, in advance of the country's parliamentary elections.

SERIES INTRODUCTION

Democracy is a form of government in which the people hold all or most of the political power. In democracies, government officials are expected to take actions and implement policies that reflect the will of the majority of the citizenry. In other political systems, the rulers generally rule for their own benefit, or at least they usually put their own interests first. This results in deep differences between the rulers and the average citizen. In undemocratic states, elites enjoy far more privileges and advantages than the average citizen. Indeed, autocratic governments are often created to exploit the average citizen.

Elections allow citizens to choose representatives to make choices for them, and under some circumstances to decide major issues themselves. Yet democracy is much more than campaigns and elections. Many nations conduct elections but are not democratic. True democracy is dependent on a range of freedoms for its citizenry, and it simultaneously exists to protect and enhance those freedoms. At its best, democracy ensures that elites, average citizens, and even groups on the margins of society all have the same rights, privileges, and opportunities. The components of democracy have changed over time as individuals and groups have struggled to expand equality. In doing so, the very notion of what makes up a democracy has evolved. The volumes in this series examine the core freedoms that form the foundation of modern democracy.

Citizenship and Immigration explores what it means to be a citizen in a democracy. The principles of democracy are based on equality, liberty, and government by the consent of the people. Equality means that all citizens have the same rights and responsibilities. Democracies have struggled to integrate all groups and ensure full equality. Citizenship in a democracy is the formal recognition that a person is a member of the country's political community. Modern democracies have faced profound debates over immigration, especially how many people to admit to the country and what rights to confer on immigrants who are not citizens.

Challenges have also emerged within democracies over how to ensure disadvantaged groups enjoy full equality with the majority, or traditionally dominant, populations. While outdated legal or political barriers have been mostly removed, democracies still struggle to overcome cultural or economic impediments to equality. *Gender Equality and Identity Rights* analyzes why gender equality has proven especially challenging, requiring political, economic, and cultural reforms. Concurrently, *Religious, Cultural, and Minority Rights* surveys the efforts that democracies have undertaken to integrate disadvantaged groups into the political, economic, and social mainstream.

A free and unfettered media provides an important check on government power and ensures an informed citizenry. The importance of free expression and a free press are detailed in *Speech, Media, and Protest*, while *Employment and Workers' Rights* provides readers with an overview of the importance of economic liberty and the ways in which employment and workers' rights reinforce equality by guaranteeing opportunity.

The maintenance of both liberty and equality requires a legal system in which the police are constrained by the rule of law. This means that security officials understand and respect the rights of individuals and groups and use their power in a manner that benefits communities, not represses them. While this is the ideal, legal systems continue to struggle to achieve equality, especially among disadvantaged groups. These topics form the core of *Justice, Policing, and the Rule of Law.*

Corruption and Transparency examines the greatest danger to democracy: corruption. Corruption can undermine people's faith in government and erode equality. Transparency, or open government, provides the best means to prevent corruption by ensuring that the decisions and actions of officials are easily understood.

As discussed in *Political Participation and Voting Rights*, a government of the people requires its citizens to provide regular input on policies and decisions through consultations and voting. Despite the importance of voting, the history of democracies has been marked by the struggle to expand voting rights. Many groups, including women, only gained the right to vote in the last century, and continue to be underrepresented in political office.

Ultimately, all of the foundations of democracy are interrelated. Equality ensures liberty, while liberty helps maintain equality. Meanwhile, both are necessary for a government by consent to be effective and lasting. Within a democracy, all people must be treated equally and be able to enjoy the full range of liberties of the country, including rights such as free speech, religion, and voting.

—Tom Lansford

CHAPTER ONE

FREEDOM OF SPEECH

 ## WORDS TO UNDERSTAND

autocracy: a system of government in which a small circle of elites holds most, if not all, political power.

Bill of Rights: the first 10 amendments to the U.S. Constitution, which protect a range of basic rights of citizens of the United States.

democracy: a system of government in which citizens hold all or most political power.

Enlightenment: a period in 17th and 18th century European history in which there were great strides made in science, philosophy, and secular political values.

freedom of expression: the right to express one's personal views publicly without fear of government penalties.

institutions: the manifestation of a country's values and norms in governmental bodies.

A statue in Paris honors the Greek statesman Pericles (495–429 BCE), whose ideas influenced our understanding of democracy.

T he right to express one's views without fear of government retribution is central to the existence of any credible **democracy**. Without the guarantee of **freedom of expression**, a society will lack the knowledge that grows out of an open exchange of ideas. By contrast, an **autocracy**, where any criticism of the ruling regime is quickly silenced, is the polar opposite of democratic governance. Countries operate along a political continuum, with democracies (such as Australia, Canada, France, Japan, and the United States) at one end, and autocracies (such as Iran, North Korea, and Russia) at the other. In the middle are countries that can move in either direction on the spectrum, depending on the political leadership and circumstances in the country at the time.

A BRIEF PRIMER ON DEMOCRACY

The history of democracy dates to Classical Greece in the fifth century BCE. Indeed, the term *democracy* is derived from the Greek words *demos* ("people") and *kratos* ("rule"). All citizens of the city-state of Athens had an opportunity to vote on the central issues of the day. The system was imperfect, as substantial segments of the population (namely, women and slaves) lacked citizenship and voting rights. But it was markedly more democratic than that of Athens's principal contemporary rival, the autocratic, military-led city-state of Sparta.

Democratic values and **institutions** under the Roman Republic (509–27 BCE) were comparable to those of Classical Greece, with a Senate that included only male citizens. But the Roman Empire (27 BCE–476 CE) was decidedly more autocratic in character. A millennium dominated predominantly by European monarchies (save for Muslim occupation and governance of much of the Iberian Peninsula, where modern Spain and Portugal are located) ensued, setting the stage for the progression of democracy during the Renaissance and Reformation.

The birth of liberal democracy can be traced to the European **Enlightenment** of the 17th and 18th centuries. Above all, the Enlightenment represented a rejection

QUOTABLE ENLIGHTENMENT

Two of the most influential philosophers of the early European Enlightenment were the Frenchman René Descartes (1596–1650) and the German Immanuel Kant (1724–1804). Considered by many to be the father of modern philosophy, Descartes is known best for one succinct statement: "*je pense, donc je suis*," which translates as "I think, therefore I am." This statement emphasized the importance of rational individual thought. In one of Kant's signature works, *Perpetual Peace: A Philosophical Sketch* (1795), he emphasizes the capacity and willingness of human beings to cooperate and build democratic societies.

A portrait of René Descartes by Jan Baptist Weenix.

of the political power and religious authority of an increasingly corrupt and widely unpopular Roman Catholic Church. What began as a protest movement against the church evolved into a broader Reformation in which "Protestant" denominations split with Catholicism. The Reformation was built on the premise that Christians had the ability to practice their faith on the basis of the Bible, without instruction from the Catholic Church on precisely how to do so. It provided the impetus for the longer-term Enlightenment agenda of secularism and democratic political reforms that undercut both papal and royal power across the continent.

The settlement of the Thirty Years' War of 1618–1648 reduced the power and influence of the Holy Roman Empire. Those changes in the political and religious landscape helped create the intellectual space needed for the gifted philosophers of the age to press for further reforms. This led to greater individual freedoms and more representative processes in governments. Prominent among such reform-minded thinkers were the Englishman John Locke (1632–1704) and the Frenchman François-Marie Arouet (1694–1778), more commonly known as Voltaire. Through works such as *An Essay Concerning Human Understanding* (1689), Locke stressed the need to make the British political system more democratic. Similarly, Voltaire advocated political reform in France and Western Europe, often through fictional works critical of existing societal norms, such as *Plato's Dream* (1756) and *Candide* (1759). Locke, Voltaire, and others helped build the foundation for democracy in France and Great Britain. Their ideas also helped inspire Britain's rebellious North American colonies, which fought a successful war for independence that resulted in the establishment of the United States.

THE POWER OF EXPRESSION

To understand the power and innate fairness of free speech, one need only consider the history of one of the contemporary world's most prominent democracies—the United States. The American colonies that formed the basis for the United States used the power of expression to launch a bid for freedom from British rule by promulgating the Declaration of Independence on July 4, 1776. After winning the American Revolutionary War in 1783, the leaders of the colonies engaged in open debate over the founding principles of the United States through the publication of a series of *Federalist Papers* and *Anti-Federalist Papers*. The debate focused on the appropriate levels of federal and state power specified in the Constitution. Those works were published between 1787 and 1788, and the Constitution of 1789 reflected a balance between the views of Federalists such as John Adams and Alexander Hamilton (1755–1804), on the one hand, and Anti-Federalists like Thomas Jefferson and James Madison, on the other.

Howard Chandler Christy's painting Scene at the Signing of the Constitution of the United States *was completed in 1940 and hangs in the House of Representatives wing of the U.S. Capitol.*

FREEDOM OF SPEECH AND DEMOCRACY IN THE WEST

The original American colonists fled Britain to pursue the right to practice their religious beliefs and achieve greater economic opportunities. So it is hardly surprising that the United States became a liberal democracy. Because they were denied political representation, the colonists made a point to ensure basic rights for future generations of Americans. Their leaders, the so-called Founding Fathers, included a range of freedoms, most notably those associated with political and religious beliefs and expression, within the first 10 amendments to the U.S. Constitution, known then and since as the **Bill of Rights**.

History has shown that that the development of enduring democratic institutions is an evolutionary process—one that moves at different speeds depending on the circumstances. For instance, for much of the history of the United States, as was true

CONTINUUM OF DEMOCRACY

As is typical of any brand of political philosophy, democracy progresses (and at times regresses) along a continuum, with the characteristics of governmental institutions evolving as events unfold. At one end of that spectrum is *liberal democracy*; at the other is *illiberal democracy*. There are two significant distinctions between these brands of political systems.

First, liberal democracy includes the necessary protections for freedom of verbal and written expression. The ability to debate and criticize the government has produced open and productive societies within (and outside of) the West. Illiberal democracy does not allow such freedom. In a number of repressive regimes that theoretically are still democracies, such as Cuba, Iran, and Russia, there is an absence of individual liberties.

Second, while liberal and illiberal democratic systems both feature regular national elections, in illiberal systems there are strict governmental controls on which candidates qualify to run, as well as state monopolies on media coverage. These controls ensure that only the political messages condoned by leaders (for instance, Cuban president Raul Castro, Iranian ayatollah Ali Khamenei, and Russian president Vladimir Putin) are heard.

Russia is technically a democracy, but some Russians argue that the government does not truly represent them. Here, residents of the city of Nizhny Novgorod rally to protest the results of an election held in December 2011.

The Freedom Monument in Riga, Latvia, was established in 1935 to honor those who fought in Latvia's War of Independence. The statue was also the center of protests against Latvia's annexation by the USSR, which ended in 1990.

of the Athenians and Romans, only white males had the right to vote. Women and slaves did not have this right. In fact, some of the Founding Fathers owned slaves. But over time, and often at great cost, the United States developed into one of the world's signature liberal democracies.

Transformative events can also prompt a sudden shift to independence, which can lead to variants of democracy in countries that escape the domination of foreign occupiers. Numerous countries in Africa, Asia, and the Middle East secured their independence from Western European colonial powers in the aftermath of World War II. Among these nations is India, the world's most populous democracy, with more than one billion people. Similarly, the end of the Cold War between the United States and the Soviet Union in 1989–1990 led to the abandonment of communism in favor of democracy in countries across Central and Eastern Europe, including the Czech Republic, Hungary, and Poland.

TEXT-DEPENDENT QUESTIONS

1. What are the most significant similarities and differences between liberal democracy and illiberal democracy?
2. What factors contributed most to the development of the European Enlightenment?
3. How is the freedom of speech addressed in the U.S. Constitution?

RESEARCH PROJECTS

1. Research the evolution of philosophical thinking on democracy and individualism during the European Enlightenment. Please summarize the central arguments of any two philosophers of this period.
2. Research the sections of the U.S. Constitution that safeguard individual freedoms. Explain why such freedoms are central to the maintenance of American democracy.

CHAPTER TWO

FREEDOM OF THE PRESS

WORDS TO UNDERSTAND

conglomerate: a large corporation made up of various parts or divisions.

journalism: objective reporting of the news on a variety of issues by a range of electronic and print media outlets.

printing press: a device used to reproduce written documents through the use of movable metal type, invented in 1440 CE.

Renaissance: A "rebirth" of diplomacy, science, and the arts in 15th and 16th century Europe.

sound bite: a catchy synopsis of a policy position designed for repetitive delivery by politicians in television interviews.

In order for a democratic political system to function in a transparent fashion, freedom of the press is essential. That guarantee, most often specified in the constitutions of liberal democratic countries, allows for the effective practice of

Great Britain has a lively newspaper tradition that dates back more than 300 years.

THE LEGACY OF THE PRINTING PRESS

When the German goldsmith Johannes Gutenberg (1395–1468) developed his printing press, he sparked a spread of ideas among generations of Europeans eager to learn and, in many cases, rebel against the existing political, religious, and social orders. The printing press allowed for a more rapid distribution of ideas during the Renaissance and Protestant Reformation that followed. In fact, the German monk Martin Luther (1483–1546), whose criticism of the Catholic Church sparked the Reformation, used the printing press to distribute works such as his *Ninety-Five Theses* (1517), which were a protest against the corruption and political machinations of the papacy in Rome.

This recreation of Gutenberg's press is on display at the International Printing Museum in Carson, California.

journalism by media outlets of various types, such as newspapers, television networks, or online sources. Rooted in the principles of individualism, rational thought, the exchange of ideas, and representative government, journalism was born in the West. However, the evolution of the mass media is by no means limited to that part of the world.

THE BASIS FOR FREEDOM OF THE PRESS

The history of the mass media began with the invention of the **printing press**. This was one of a number of significant developments in science and the humanities during the European **Renaissance** of the 15th and 16th centuries. The development of a printing press based on the use of movable metal type, invented by Johannes Gutenberg in 1440, provided a means for the faster and wider distribution of the latest ideas in many disciplines, including astronomy, mathematics, medicine, history, philosophy, and politics. These ideas, and the intellectual and scientific advancement accompanying them, represented the very core of the purpose of the media, both then and now: to inform the public.

Europe's first newspapers date to the 17th century. The continent's first weekly newspaper, *Relation*, was published in Antwerp, Belgium, in 1605. The first English-language daily, the *Daily Courant*, began in 1702. A few of the prominent 18th century national newspapers are still in print in the United Kingdom today, including the *Daily Universal Register* (founded in 1785, it was renamed the *Times* three years later) and the *Observer*, from 1791.

The emergence of freedom of expression and, more pointedly, the press, developed gradually in Western Europe over a period of centuries. It began with the Protestant Reformation of the 16th century, continued during the 17th and 18th century European Enlightenment, and culminated with the establishment of European democracies in the 19th century. Along the way, philosophers used the printing press to spread their views on a variety of topics, including opposition to the authority of the Catholic Church and rejection of autocratic governance.

The defeat of one of those empires, Napoleon Bonaparte's France in 1815, helped create an environment more conducive to the establishment of newspapers. In turn, those papers exerted greater pressure for political reform, which eventually spread to the colonies of the British, French, and Spanish in North and South America. After the founding of the United States, former colonies across Latin America declared their independence from European powers over the first quarter of the 18th century. Argentina, Chile, and Colombia declared their independence from Spain in 1816, 1818, and 1819, respectively, and Brazil declared its independence from Portugal in 1822.

After risking their lives by signing the Declaration of Independence on July 4, 1776, the Founding Fathers of the United States were determined to ensure that future generations of Americans would be guaranteed the fundamental rights denied to the inhabitants of the 13 colonies. This required the development of a citizenry that was informed about events and issues that affected them on a daily basis. They also had to be exposed to a variety of viewpoints, including some critical of the government in power. The first of the 10 amendments to the U.S. Constitution, known collectively as the Bill of Rights, guaranteed freedom of expression, including freedom of the press. Those values were comparable to the ones evolving across the Atlantic world at the time. And similar reform processes unfolded within Western Europe after World War II, and in Central and Eastern Europe following the end of the Cold War. Among the earliest instances of the establishment of freedom of the press in European countries were in Britain in 1689 and France in 1789.

THE EVOLUTION OF WESTERN MEDIA

The media has evolved considerably over the centuries. The process began with the establishment and expansion of a vibrant newspaper industry in the 19th century, both in Western Europe and North America. Among the most prominent national newspapers in American colonial history were the weekly *Boston News-Letter* (1704), *Boston Gazette* (1719), and *New-York Gazette* (1725). Daily newspapers began appearing in the aftermath of the Revolutionary War, with notable examples including the *New York Sun* (1833) and *New York Herald* (1833). As the industry expanded and profits rose, leading publishers, including Joseph Pulitzer (1847–1911) and William Randolph Hearst (1863–1951), waged circulation battles between their flagship newspapers: Pulitzer's *New York World* and Hearst's *New York Morning Journal* and *New York Evening Journal*.

Competition drove expansion in newspaper readership through sensationalistic reporting, which critics branded as "yellow journalism." This approach helped President William McKinley gain public support for the Spanish-American War, which began on the basis an inaccurate report of a bomb sinking the USS *Maine* in the harbor of Havana, the capital of Spain's Cuban colony, in February 1898. In reality, the ship sank as the result of a mechanical failure, which caused an explosion in the ship's boiler room. Nonetheless, the United States attacked Spain and scored a resounding victory.

American newspaper magnates such as Pulitzer and Hearst contributed to a monopoly of sorts for the print media in reporting the news to the U.S. public. However, as is true of

This famous cartoon from 1898 satirizes the way competing newspapers owned by Joseph Pulitzer and William Randolph Hearst pushed public opinion toward war with Spain.

A portrait of editor Joseph Pulitzer, framed by his famous paper. The Pulitzer Prizes for excellence in journalism were established by Pulitzer and have been awarded since 1917.

most businesses, that monopoly did not last forever. By the 1920s, boosted by the invention of the telegraph, radio networks had begun to create a much more competitive environment for the previously unchallenged publishing **conglomerates**. Among these networks was the British Broadcasting Company (BBC), which rapidly expanded service throughout the United Kingdom's global empire. For many, simply switching on the radio was more

 ## THE EVOLUTION OF BROADCAST NEWS

As with any industry, broadcast journalism has evolved considerably over time. It began with the invention of the wireless radio telegraph by the Italian physicist Guglielmo Marconi (1874–1937) in 1899. The first successful transatlantic electronic communication occurred two years later. It expanded through the proliferation of radio networks in the 1920s and 1930s. And it culminated in the decisions of executives at American and Western European national radio networks to add television operations in the 1940s and 1950s. These developments paved the way to the globalization of the media, which is covered in depth in chapter three.

Listening to the radio with headphones, circa 1920.

convenient than reading the newspaper. And one could find out what happened right away, instead of waiting for the next edition of the local paper to arrive.

Radio stations were themselves eclipsed by the advent of the television news network in the 1940s and 1950s, including the national "big three," ABC, CBS, and NBC. These were followed by cable and satellite television stations in later decades. Parallels can be drawn to the publishing industry in the United Kingdom, particularly with respect to the BBC, which has both radio and television components. The emergence and expansion of the Internet as a means of rapid information exchange has contributed further to an environment in which the 30-second **sound bite** is the preferred style of political communication.

TEXT-DEPENDENT QUESTIONS

1. How did the invention of the printing press affect the communication of ideas during the Protestant Reformation and European Enlightenment of the 17th and 18th centuries?

2. In what ways are newspapers and television networks similar? In what ways are they dissimilar?

3. In what ways has the evolution of broadcast television news networks affected the ways politicians run campaigns and carry out their duties while in office?

RESEARCH PROJECTS

1. Research the evolution of the media over the course of American history. Identify and assess the implications of three innovations of your choice on the media industry in the United States.

2. Research the relationship between the media and politics. Assess the effects of technological improvements on that relationship during a historical period of your choice.

CHAPTER THREE

GLOBALIZATION OF THE MEDIA

 WORDS TO UNDERSTAND

globalization: a trend toward increased interconnectedness between nations and cultures across the world; globalization impacts the spheres of politics, economics, culture, and mass media.

intrastate: within the boundaries of a particular state or nation.

social media: Internet-based communications that link individuals across the world via devices, such as smartphones, computers, and tablets.

The end of the Cold War in 1991 signaled the start of a new historical period. A signature component of the post–Cold War era is the phenomenon of **globalization**, which has exposed an increasing proportion of the world's peoples to information about others, primarily through enhancements in communications technology. Such enhancements have been especially beneficial to media outlets that broadcast news globally over cable and satellite television networks.

GLOBALIZATION AND THE MEDIA

Globalization has had significant effects on industries in countries around the world, including the mass media. By exposing a progressively broader proportion of the earth's population to information about the world than was previously the case, the Internet has created a global demand for news of all types. In addition, news is now continuously updated throughout the day. Among the issue areas that globalization has affected most are culture, economics, politics, religion, and security—all of which influence the behavior of individuals, countries, and organizations. The interest of individuals in the roles of governments and institutions has increased, primarily because of increased access to information through a vast array of mass media sources.

Globalization has dramatically changed the very meaning of the "media." While technological innovations have long driven the evolution of the media (as discussed in chapter two), the globalization of the post–Cold War era has been distinctive in two

 ## THE RISE OF GLOBAL INTERNET USERS

As the following figures illustrate, the number of global Internet users grew markedly over the last quarter of the 20th century. Much of that growth has come in the developing world, where the two most populous countries on earth, China and India, are situated.

Year	Internet users (millions)	Percent of global population with Internet
1995	44.8	0.8%
2000	413.4	6.7%
2005	1,029.7	15.8%
2010	2,034.3	29.4%
2014 (July 1)	2,925.3	40.4%

Source: Internet Live States, http://www.internetlivestats.com/internet-users/#trend.

Outside an Internet café in Fez, Morocco.

A man selling newspapers in Yangon, Myanmar, in 2013.

ways. First, it developed during the start of an era characterized by uncertainty in the international system. There was a dramatic increase in the number of wars, for one thing, including **intrastate** conflicts. These conflicts were driven largely by ethnic, racial, religious, and tribal factors in parts of the developing world, particularly as globalization highlighted inequalities in wealth and in economic and social development. People in less developed nations increasingly advocated for improvements in their standard of living and a greater say in government. In 2011, for example, a series of revolutions toppled long-time dictators in the Middle East and North Africa, in what became known as the Arab Spring. Unfortunately, many of these revolutions led to continuing strife or new dictatorial regimes.

Second, globalization helped shape the era in revolutionary ways that few would have anticipated. These developments involved the stories the media had to report as well as the tools at the disposal of media networks and reporters. For example, global cable television networks used technological improvements to expose viewers to the humanitarian costs of intrastate conflicts, including the civil wars of the 1990s in southeastern Europe. This eventually led to military intervention by the North Atlantic Treaty Organization (NATO) in Bosnia-Herzegovina in the summer and fall of 1995, and in Kosovo in the spring of 1999.

THE PROLIFERATION OF GLOBAL TELEVISION NEWS NETWORKS

The global cable television news industry traces its origins to the birth of CNN, which was established by Ted Turner, the owner of the Turner Broadcasting Company, in June 1980. Many in the broadcast news industry were skeptical about Turner's idea, wondering how CNN could fill 24 hours of time every day with compelling stories. Turner proved his critics wrong. Initially available in just 2 million American homes, a marginal figure in a market dominated by the national nightly news broadcasts of ABC, CBS, and NBC, CNN's 24-hour format quickly drove demand upward. It can now be seen in some 89 million American homes, and in more than 160 million homes internationally.

After dominating the cable news market for the first 15 years of its existence, CNN began to draw significant competition, particularly from MSNBC and the Fox News Network, both of which began broadcasting in 1996. The three networks spanned the political spectrum, with MSNBC on the left, CNN a bit closer to the center, and Fox on the right. Collectively, they helped boost cable television subscriptions from 17.7 million in 1980 to 44.5 million in 2010. Examples of comparable global cable and satellite television networks include Sky News in London, Deutsche Welle in Berlin, France 24 in Paris, and Al Jazeera and Al Arabiya in the Middle East.

A signature moment in CNN's transformation of the television news industry to one emphasizing instantaneous coverage of important events was that network's coverage of the opening night of the Persian Gulf War on January 17–18, 1991. As bombs rained down on the Iraqi capital of Baghdad at the start of Operation Desert Storm (which ultimately achieved its objective of forcing President Saddam Hussein's forces from the neighboring state of Kuwait, which they had invaded in August 1990), CNN newsmen Bernard Shaw and Peter Arnett broadcast what amounted to a live play-by-play of the ongoing events from their hotel room in the city.

Inside CNN's world headquarters in Atlanta, Georgia.

In subsequent years and decades, the brand of captivating live coverage Shaw and Arnett provided that night has become the rule rather than the exception. One harrowing and poignant example of such coverage came on September 11, 2001, when al-Qaeda operatives hijacked four passenger airliners, crashing two into the north and south towers of the World Trade Center in New York and a third into the Pentagon in Arlington, Virginia, before the passengers aboard the fourth forced the terrorists to crash it into a field in Shanksville, Pennsylvania. More recent cases of such coverage include terrorist attacks carried out by Islamist extremists in Madrid in March 2004, London in July 2005, and Paris in both January and November 2015.

SOCIAL MEDIA AND THE NEWS

The emergence and expansion of **social media** in the 21st century has had a significant effect on gathering and reporting the news. Social media networks afford individuals the opportunity to collect information as events occur, whether related to culture, economics, ethnicity, politics, security, social class, religion, or a variety of other matters. Essentially, an individual can be both part of an unfolding story *and* a conveyor of that story. Social media networks provide American television networks such as CNN, the Fox News Channel, and MSNBC, as well those headquartered in other parts of the world, such as Sky News, Al Jazeera, and Al Arabiya, with access to developing aspects of a story they would not otherwise be able to communicate to their viewers. Text, audio, and video accounts of the news can then be uploaded to a social media network such as Facebook, Twitter, or YouTube via a smartphone.

Social media has come of age alongside many of the signature events of the 2000s and 2010s, whether related to domestic politics in a given country or to crises and conflicts in the international system. Several related events in the Middle East illustrate the increasingly interconnected relationship between social media networks and the global news media.

Social media sites like Twitter have sparked a revolution in how, where, and when people get their news.

First, in June 2009, in the aftermath of the re-election of Iranian president Mahmoud Ahmadinejad, thousands of protesters took to the streets of Tehran to protest what they perceived as electoral fraud by the Iranian regime. When that regime used its security forces to crush the rebellion, the global exposure of its actions was far greater than would have otherwise been the case, thanks to the protesters' ability to post video accounts of the carnage via social media.

Then, this phenomenon spread when a series of protests sprang up against economic problems and governmental repression by regimes across the Middle East in 2010–2011, known since as the Arab Spring. While the former case did little to reduce the power

SOCIAL MEDIA AND POLITICS

Since the 1990s, the Internet has revolutionized the ways in which (and the speeds at which) human beings communicate. The need to communicate effectively to current (and prospective new) supporters has always been critically important to political campaigning. The most recent additions to Internet-based outreach include the ever-growing pool of globally accessible social media networks, most notably Facebook and Twitter, but also Instagram, Periscope, and Snapchat.

Consequently, it is hardly surprisingly that politicians campaigning for office at the national, regional, and local levels throughout the developed world boast Facebook pages and Twitter handles, with followers equating to votes in a given election. Numerous leaders around the world have Twitter pages, including American president Barack Obama, British prime minister David Cameron, French president Francois Hollande, and Russian president Vladimir Putin.

Indian Prime Minister Narendra Modi (@Narendra Modi) had 12 million Twitter followers in 2015. He was the third most-followed world leader on Twitter; President Barack Obama (@BarackObama) was first with around 60 million followers, and Pope Francis (@pontifex) was second, with about 20 million followers.

of the Iranian regime, the latter led to the removal from power of a number of Middle Eastern autocrats, including Egyptian president Hosni Mubarak and Libyan leader Muammar Qaddafi.

TEXT-DEPENDENT QUESTIONS

1. How has globalization affected the reporting of the news across the world since the 1990s?

2. What factors have driven the proliferation of 24-hour television news networks since the end of the Cold War?

3. How have social media networks such as Facebook and Twitter affected politics?

RESEARCH PROJECTS

1. Research the evolution of globalization. Assess the effects of globalization on media coverage of a conflict of your choice since 1991.

2. Research the development of Internet-based social media networks. Assess the effects of such networks on domestic politics on a country of your choice since the start of the 21st century.

CHAPTER FOUR

FREEDOM OF EXPRESSION AND PROTEST

 ## WORDS TO UNDERSTAND

civil rights: government-protected liberties afforded to people of all ethnicities, genders, and races in democratic countries.

interest groups: clusters of individuals united by (and committed to) advocacy on the basis of a common position on a particular issue.

nongovernmental organization (NGO): an organization whose members do not include governmental bodies or representatives of such bodies.

nonstate actors: individuals or groups, including businesses, civic organizations, and interest groups, that have an influence in politics and society but are not formal components of a national government.

oligarchy: a country in which political power is held by a small, powerful, but unelected group of leaders.

A Syrian woman living in Turkey joins in a protest against the dictator Bashar al Assad.

I n liberal democratic societies, there is often an interdependent relationship between national governments and protest movements. This situation arose for two reasons. First, in order for the members of any group to express their views publicly without fear of retaliatory action, physical or otherwise, the government of the country in which they reside must guarantee the freedom of expression needed for protests to occur. Second, for a country to be a credible liberal democracy, it must ensure the right of its citizens to express their views, including criticism of the government. Without these protected liberties, a country cannot be a true democracy.

INTERDEPENDENCE BETWEEN GOVERNANCE AND DISSENT

At its core, the relationship between governments and their citizens is an interdependent one, whether the political system in place is an **oligarchy** or a democracy. In the former case, the regime in charge must gauge accurately how much power—economic, military, political, or otherwise—is needed to prevent a successful takeover attempt. Examples of oligarchies range from the family-dominated dictatorships of the Assads in Syria and the Kims in North Korea at one end of the autocratic spectrum, to illiberal democracies like Belarus and Venezuela at the other. The military and political dominance of oligarchies renders resistance dangerous, with imprisonment or death awaiting those who dare to resist.

In true democracies, by contrast, accountability and power are driven by the electoral system, with voters afforded the opportunity to elect a challenger or re-elect an incumbent president or prime minister every four or five years. Examples of these types of liberal democracies include Australia, Canada, France, Japan, and the United States.

The relationship between political dissent and democracy is complicated. The level of tolerance for protest movements often differs from one historical period to another. One of the earliest and most historically relevant examples of successful political and religious dissent was the Protestant Reformation of 16th and 17th century Europe.

This protest movement resulted in various Protestant strains of Christianity splintering away from Catholicism. Political dissent also drove the evolution of modern liberal democratic political systems in the West. For instance, women did not gain the right to vote until protest movements pressured governments in the late 1800s and early 1900s.

PROTEST MOVEMENTS

Protest movements have a rich history in Western civilization. The late 18th century was punctuated by protests against British rule by its colonies along the eastern seaboard of North America. The Declaration of Independence of July 4, 1776, represented as strong an act of protest as imaginable, sparking the American Revolution, which ended in a colonial victory in 1783, leading to the establishment of the United States and the ratification of the Constitution in 1789. Midway through the 19th century, the Revolutions of 1848 marked the beginning of the end of meaningful political authority of royal families across Europe, most notably in places such as Austria-Hungary.

The fundamental rights and liberties built into the U.S. Constitution have provided fertile ground for protest movements. It began with a protest against federal liquor taxes during the first term of the inaugural American president, George Washington (1732–1799). This grew into the violent Whiskey Rebellion, which was forcibly put down in 1792. And it continued in earnest under President Barack H. Obama (1961–), as evidenced by the efforts of grassroots protest groups, including the conservative Tea Party, the Occupy Wall Street movement against economic inequality, and the Black Lives Matter movement.

In between, African-American hopes for improvements in the extent of **civil rights** afforded to them came to fruition amid the protests of the 1960s. Most prominent among those who drove the civil rights movement forward was the Rev. Dr. Martin Luther King Jr. (1929–1968), a Baptist preacher who advocated nonviolent protest as a path to political and social change. Similarly, the final act of the Cold War was sparked in part by the development of peaceful protest movements opposing Soviet-supported regimes across

Protesters at the March on Washington for Jobs and Freedom, on August 28, 1963. Dr. Martin Luther King Jr. delivered his historic "I Have a Dream" speech at this gathering of about 250,000 people in Washington, D.C.

SOLIDARITY AND THE END OF THE COLD WAR

All revolutions are fueled to at least some extent by protest movements. That was certainly the case for the Solidarity movement of the 1980s in Poland, which contributed significantly to the end of the communist regimes that were imposed on the countries of Central and Eastern Europe by the Soviet Union throughout the Cold War. Founded by Lech Walesa (1943–) in the shipyards of the Baltic Sea port of Gdansk in September 1980, the labor union called Solidarność (Solidarity) prompted a crackdown by the Soviets that ultimately proved unsuccessful. By 1989, Solidarność had helped spark similar protest movements across the region, the end result of which was the end of the Cold War. For his part, Walesa was elected as Poland's first post-communist president, a position he held from 1990 to 1995.

Solidarność is Polish for "Solidarity."

Central and Eastern Europe, the most successful of which included the Solidarity labor union in Poland and the Velvet Revolution in Czechoslovakia.

NGOs, Advocacy, and Global Interests

Since the end of the Cold War, **nongovernmental organizations** (NGOs) have seen an extraordinary increase in both their number and the extent of their influence on domestic and international politics. The globalization process has played a central role in enhancing the influence of **interest groups** across a broad range of issue areas, primarily because of the ways that the process enhances communications and unites individuals with compatible views.

The connections fostered by globalization are not limited to links between any particular sets of individuals or groups, nor are there any set geographical limits to its capacity to cultivate collaborative thinking and spread ideas. Where limits do appear, they grow primarily out of the imposition of limits by autocratic governments and leaders fearful of the ways that the open exchange of information can undermine their political

 NGOS IN INDIA

Since the end of the Cold War, the number of NGOs in India has grown faster than in any other country. This is mainly the result of a lack of government services. NGOs in the country are created to serve needs that are unfilled by the government in areas such as health care, education, and economic development. For instance, some NGOs operate clinics or hospitals, while others provide loans or grants to establish new businesses. According to the *Times of India*, in 2014, India, with a population of 1.2 billion people, had an estimated 2 million NGOs, or one for every 600 people. In comparison, the nation had one policeman for every 943 people.

In London, protesters organized by Amnesty International stand outside the U.S. embassy to decry the U.S. policy of holding detainees at the Guantanamo Bay detention camp.

authority. Such regimes typically respond by imposing whatever controls they can on access to the Internet, and by punishing anyone who manages to gain access anyway. Notable examples around the world include China and Saudi Arabia, but even nominal democracies such as Turkey sometimes limit access to online information deemed to be harmful or critical of the regime.

In recent decades, the Internet has evolved into a globally accessible and influential way for individuals to communicate across previously existing barriers. Indeed, the Internet has served as a nearly perfect tool for **nonstate actors** to refine and spread their messages. This is true for all types of such actors, whether they are involved in noble or nefarious causes, and whether they are local, national, or international in scope.

At the local level, community activists regularly use the Internet to pass along information on (and gain support for) particular stances or programs. At the national level, interest groups use enhanced communications to try to influence the political process, with illustrative cases including actors with goals as varied as the Second Amendment–based National Rifle Association and the environmentally friendly Sierra Club. Globally, watchdog groups use the Internet to cast light on leaders who use the regimes they control to deny their citizens basic political rights and economic

Antigovernment demonstration in Tahir Square, Cairo. During the Arab Spring protests, activists used social media to publicize their cause.

opportunities, or to build vast personal fortunes. Notable examples include Amnesty International, Human Rights Watch, and Transparency International. Where these groups' causes are noble, others seek enhanced power for radical purposes, as is the case with violent religious extremist organizations such as al-Qaeda and the Islamic State of Iraq and Syria (ISIS), which are examined in greater depth in chapter five.

TEXT-DEPENDENT QUESTIONS

1. What role did protests play in the establishment of the United States?
2. How did protest movements affect the end of the Cold War?
3. What factors have contributed most to the proliferation of NGOs across the world since the 1990s?

RESEARCH PROJECTS

1. Research the history of protest movements. Assess the factors that contributed most to the genesis of protest movements associated with at least one issue in the country of your choice since the start of the 20th century.
2. Research the development of nongovernmental organizations focusing on an issue area of your choice. Assess the factors that have contributed most to the political influence exercised by this NGO since the start of the 21st century.

CHAPTER FIVE

BALANCING SECURITY AND CIVIL LIBERTIES

 ## WORDS TO UNDERSTAND

civil liberties: freedoms associated with the right to political expression, especially in liberal democracies.

electronic surveillance: the monitoring of communications by individuals, governments, and countries for a variety of national security and law enforcement purposes.

flash mob: the sudden appearance of a group of protestors at a given site, typically in response to recruitment through online social media networks.

homeland security: threats to the domestic territory of a country and the means to counter such dangers.

terrorism: organized violence against civilian or military targets designed to achieve political objectives.

violent extremism: attacks committed by an individual or group against others in support of a radical political or religious ideology.

On September 11, 2001, a violent Islamic extremist organization known as al-Qaeda carried out a series of terrorist attacks against the United States, killing nearly 3,000 people. Those attacks, the deadliest acts of **terrorism** in American history, triggered President George W. Bush's declaration of a "global war on terror." Central to the domestic front was congressional passage of the Patriot Act (officially, the USA PATRIOT Act) of October 2001. The act enhanced the extent of **electronic surveillance** tools at the disposal of American federal law enforcement and **homeland security** agencies and departments in the struggle against terrorist organizations such as al-Qaeda. It also raised significant concerns among **civil liberties** groups, however.

An informal memorial to the people killed during the terror attack on Paris in November 2015.

PROVISIONS OF THE USA PATRIOT ACT AFFECTING CIVIL LIBERTIES

Passed by Congress and signed into law by President George W. Bush in October 2001, the Uniting and Strengthening America by Providing Appropriate Tools Required to Intercept and Obstruct Terrorism (USA PATRIOT) Act includes the following legal provisions that have drawn consistent criticism from American civil liberties advocacy groups:

1. The collection of "metadata" telephone records from American citizens deemed useful by the National Security Agency (NSA) in the struggle against foreign-based terrorist organizations, most notably al-Qaeda and its affiliates and rivals, and store that data for up to five years.

2. The use of roving wiretaps to track terrorist groups, whose members frequently change portable communications devices, particularly cell phones, in an effort to elude detection by U.S. law enforcement agencies.

3. The use of "national security" tools to track suspected "lone wolf" terrorists in the United States, even if a direct link to a violent extremist organization cannot be secured beforehand.

TERRORISM, CIVIL LIBERTIES, AND GOVERNANCE

In the aftermath of the tragic events of 9/11, the Bush administration moved to put in place legal and policy tools designed to uncover, counter, and preclude any comparable terrorist attacks in the future. Those tools, which have been employed both by Bush and his successor, President Barack H. Obama, feature domestic and international components, many of which parallel measures put in place by Western European states following terrorist attacks there, such as the bombings of the Madrid and London public transportation systems, in March 2004 and July 2005, respectively. The tools of greatest importance on the homeland security front of the war on terror are those associated with the use of electronic surveillance tools to track the activities of al-Qaeda, the Islamic State of Iraq and Syria (ISIS), and other extremist groups.

Throughout history, one can identify instances where countries have erred on the side of strong security measures at home in the face of pronounced national security threats. In most (though certainly not all) cases, one can make a pragmatic argument for measures that complicate the civil liberties afforded to the populace in some way. However, there are also examples of instances where Western democracies took actions that produced significant criticism, particularly in hindsight, as

The Irish navy rescues a boat of migrants as part of Operation Triton.

CIVIL LIBERTIES IN PERSPECTIVE: DEMOCRACY VERSUS AUTOCRACY

When one discusses the issue of civil liberties, it is important to maintain the proper perspective, particularly with respect to differences in the meaning of that term in democratic versus autocratic countries. In the West, for example, some government surveillance techniques have come under increased scrutiny, especially since the start of the 21st century. The liberal democratic values and laws entrenched in these societies ensure the right to criticize and call for a tempering, if not elimination, of such provisions. In more autocratic states, a single act of protest often means imprisonment or death. Examples of political prisoners held for their human rights advocacy include the prominent Chinese scholar Liu Xiaobo, Iranian activists Omid Alishenas and Asou Rostami, and Azerbaijani activists Leyla and Arif Yunus.

historians cast judgment on a given period. One example came in the aftermath of the Japanese surprise attack against the American Pacific fleet at Pearl Harbor on December 7, 1941. In response, as the United States entered World War II, the administration of President Franklin D. Roosevelt relocated more than 100,000 Japanese Americans into internment camps throughout that conflict, arguing that these detentions would prevent attacks at home. That decision has been severely criticized in the years since then.

BALANCING SECURITY AND CIVIL LIBERTIES IN THE POST-9/11 ERA

As explained above, unfolding events threatening the security of the American homeland have created the need to strike a balance between civil liberties and the safety of the populace. Typically, the more time that has elapsed since one or more defining acts of violence, the more challenging it becomes to retain national support for constrictions on individual freedoms in favor of collective security. That trend certainly holds true with respect to the U.S. and European domestic responses to terrorist attacks by Islamic extremists during the 2000s and 2010s. The passage of laws allowing law enforcement agencies and counterterrorism forces more tools to confront terrorist groups usually comes quickly as societal security concerns rise. However, that does not guarantee a perpetual willingness of the majority of the public to support measures that may help keep a country safe from terrorist attacks, but that also collect information from ordinary individuals' computers, tablets, and smartphones. Over time, concerns about such programs typically grow increasingly pronounced.

Opposition to the Patriot Act, for example, grew as memories of al-Qaeda's catastrophic attacks faded and the Bush administration intervened to remove the regime of Iraqi president Saddam Hussein in March 2003, in an effort to eliminate weapons of mass destruction that never actually materialized. The conduct of Operation Iraqi Freedom was followed by a 2003–2011 occupation that took the lives of nearly 5,000 U.S. servicemen and women, cost more than $1 trillion, and helped produce a wave of anti-Americanism abroad and antigovernment movements at home.

To be sure, such movements included people upset with the Bush administration over both the intervention in Iraq and the Patriot Act that preceded it. However, societal discontent ran much deeper and outlasted the Bush administration. While President Obama was elected on a platform of promises to end the war in Iraq and improve America's image abroad, his administration maintained the domestic surveillance programs instituted by Bush, drawing criticism from civil liberties advocates on both sides of the political spectrum. Some of these groups have used social media outlets to produce **flash mobs** to protest over various issues.

Activists have put a sticker on this payphone to protest what they see as unjustifiable spying on the communications of citizens. The sticker reads in part: "Your conversation is being monitored by the U.S. Government courtesy of the US Patriot Act of 2001, Sec. 216 of which permits all phone calls to be recorded without a warrant or notification."

JULIAN ASSANGE

Activists who are concerned about what they perceive to be civil liberties abuses frequently highlight the use of electronic surveillance programs to collect data on the activities of a country's citizens, or on other countries in the international system. Few are as well known as Julian Assange (1971–), who used electronic technology to intercept messages regarding intelligence gathering and policymaking in powerful countries, most notably the United States. Assange, an Australian with an aptitude for computer hacking and a zeal for investigative journalism, founded WikiLeaks, a website that "leaks" its findings, in 2006. Assange is also known for his legal problems. Wanted on charges of sexual assault charges in Sweden, he sought and received political asylum at the Ecuadorian embassy in London in June 2012, and he has been there ever since.

Julian Assange.

VIOLENT EXTREMISM, PROTEST GROUPS, AND DEMOCRACY: WHAT LIES AHEAD?

Above all, the 9/11 terrorist attacks signaled a troubling escalation of the dangers posed to the United States and the West by **violent extremism**. The evolution of such threats has followed three related paths. First, the American prosecution of Operation Enduring Freedom in Afghanistan in the fall of 2001 both removed the Taliban from power and forced al-Qaeda's core leadership across the border into Pakistan, reducing its capacity to plan and carry out more operations like the 9/11 attacks. It also came with broader NATO efforts to build democratic political institutions in Afghanistan.

Second, al-Qaeda adapted to the changing strategic conditions it faced by encouraging, if not directly engineering, the development of affiliated groups such as al-Qaeda in Iraq and al-Qaeda in the Arabian Peninsula, as well as smaller terrorist cells within Western Muslim communities. It was these small cells that carried out bombings of the train and subway systems in Madrid in March 2004 and London in July 2005. Third, and worst of all, a new type of Islamic extremist organization, one with broader appeal among younger generations of Muslims in the Middle East and the West, arose amid the political instability produced by Arab reform movements in 2010–2011. This was the Islamic State of Iraq and Syria (ISIS).

ISIS is distinctive from al-Qaeda and its affiliates in two ways. First, while those groups are all anti-Western and spread extreme interpretations of Islam, ISIS has grown at an alarming rate compared to the terrorist groups that preceded it. From the start of 2014 to the end of 2015, ISIS grew from several thousand fighters to more than 30,000, largely through its ability to recruit embittered young Muslims from more than 100 countries. Second, unlike previous Islamic extremist groups, ISIS has demonstrated the ability to hold large swaths of territory in Iraq and Syria. It operates more like a state than a terrorist organization, albeit one whose methods are as brutal and barbaric as the worst of the world's past dictatorships.

As of 2015, none of ISIS's Western or Middle Eastern opponents had been able to significantly reduce the power and influence of ISIS. However, that does not mean such opponents are not trying. In the aftermath of a series of terrorist attacks carried out by ISIS in Paris in November 2015, President Francois Hollande requested and received from the French Parliament a series of measures granting the government significantly increased powers to detain suspected terrorists and search and seize their property.

TEXT-DEPENDENT QUESTIONS

1. How did the 9/11 terrorist attacks affect traditional civil liberties in democracies?
2. To what extent does the Patriot Act strike a reasonable balance between homeland security safeguards and civil liberties protections?
3. What violent extremist groups present the most significant security threats in the 2010s?

RESEARCH PROJECTS

1. Research the establishment and evolution of the U.S. Department of Homeland Security. Assess the strengths and weaknesses of the department from a civil liberties perspective.
2. Research the evolution of the ISIS. Assess this violent organization's use of extreme, perverted interpretations of Islam to recruit members and sympathizers in the West.

FURTHER READING

Books

Cohen, David B., and John W. Wells, ed., *American National Security and Civil Liberties in an Era of Terrorism*. New York: Palgrave Macmillan, 2004.

Fukuyama, Francis. *The End of History and the Last Man*. New York: Free Press, 1992.

Lule, Jack. *Globalization and Media: Global Village of Babel*. 2nd ed. Lanham, MD: Rowman and Littlefield, 2015.

Pettegree, Andrew. *The Invention of News: How the World Came to Know About Itself*. New Haven, CT: Yale University Press, 2014.

Tocqueville, Alexis de. *Democracy in America*. Edited by Isaac Kramnick. Translated by Gerard Bevan. New York: Penguin Classics, 2003.

Online

Freedom House. https://www.freedomhouse.org.

Media Research Center. http://www.mrc.org.

Reporters Without Borders. http://en.rsf.org/.

Transparency International. https://www.transparency.org.

Yale Center for the Study of Globalization. http://gsnetwork.igloogroups.org/particip/members/yalecent.

SERIES GLOSSARY

accountability: making elected officials and government workers answerable to the public for their actions, and holding them responsible for mistakes or crimes.

amnesty: a formal reprieve or pardon for people accused or convicted of committing crimes.

anarchist: a person who believes that government should be abolished because it enslaves or otherwise represses people.

assimilation: the process through which immigrants adopt the cultural, political, and social beliefs of a new nation.

autocracy: a system of government in which a small circle of elites holds most, if not all, political power.

belief: an acceptance of a statement or idea concerning a religion or faith.

citizenship: formal recognition that an individual is a member of a political community.

civil law: statutes and rules that govern private rights and responsibilities and regulate noncriminal disputes over issues such as property or contracts.

civil rights: government-protected liberties afforded to all people in democratic countries.

civil servants: people who work for the government, not including elected officials or members of the military.

corruption: illegal or unethical behavior on the part of officials who abuse their position.

democracy: A government in which the people hold all or most political power and express their preferences on issues through regular voting and elections.

deportation: the legal process whereby undocumented immigrants or those who have violated residency laws are forced to leave their new country.

dual citizenship: being a full citizen of two or more countries.

election: the process of selecting people to serve in public office through voting.

expatriate: someone who resides in a country other than his or her nation of birth.

feminism: the belief in social, economic, and political equality for women.

gender rights: providing access to equal rights for all members of a society regardless of their gender.

glass ceiling: obstacles that prevent the advancement of disadvantaged groups from obtaining senior positions of authority in business, government, and education.

globalization: a trend toward increased interconnectedness between nations and cultures across the world; globalization impacts the spheres of politics, economics, culture, and mass media.

guest workers: citizens of one country who have been granted permission to temporarily work in another nation.

homogenous: a region or nation where most people have the same ethnicity, language, religion, customs, and traditions.

human rights: rights that everyone has, regardless of birthplace or citizenship.

incumbent: an official who currently holds office.

industrialization: the transformation of social life resulting from the technological and economic developments involving factories.

jurisdiction: the official authority to administer justice through activities such as investigations, arrests, and obtaining testimony.

minority: a group that is different—ethnically, racially, culturally, or in terms of religion—within a larger society.

national security: the combined efforts of a country to protect its citizens and interests from harm.

naturalization: the legal process by which a resident noncitizen becomes a citizen of a country.

nongovernmental organization (NGO): a private, nonprofit group that provides services or attempts to influence governments and international organizations.

oligarchy: a country in which political power is held by a small, powerful, but unelected group of leaders.

partisanship: a strong bias or prejudice toward one set of beliefs that often results in an unwillingness to compromise or accept alternative points of view.

refugees: people who are kicked out of their country or forced to flee to another country because they are not welcome or fear for their lives.

right-to-work laws: laws in the United States that forbid making union membership a condition for employment.

secular state: governments that are not officially influenced by religion in making decisions.

sexism: system of beliefs, or ideology, that asserts the inferiority of one sex and justifies discrimination based on gender.

socialist: describes a political system in which major businesses or industries are owned or regulated by the community instead of by individuals or privately owned companies.

socioeconomic status: the position of a person within society, based on the combination of their income, wealth, education, family background, and social standing.

sovereignty: supreme authority over people and geographic space. National governments have sovereignty over their citizens and territory.

theocracy: a system of government in which all major decisions are made under the guidance of religious leaders' interpretation of divine authority.

treason: the betrayal of one's country.

tyranny: rule by a small group or single person.

veto: the ability to reject a law or other measure enacted by a legislature.

wage gap: the disparity in earnings between men and women for their work.

INDEX

ABOUT THE AUTHOR

Dr. Robert J. Pauly, Jr. is Tenured Associate Professor of International Development at The University of Southern Mississippi. His research interests focus broadly on the fields of U.S. foreign policy, national security and homeland security, with emphases on American policy toward the states of the Greater Middle East and the evolving relationships between states and non-state actors in the Muslim and Western worlds. He is the author or co-author and editor or co-editor of seven books and more than 45 academic articles, essays and book chapters, including, most recently, *The New Islamic State: Ideology, Religion and Violent Extremism in the 21st Century* (2016).

ABOUT THE ADVISOR

Tom Lansford is a Professor of Political Science, and a former academic dean, at the University of Southern Mississippi, Gulf Coast. He is a member of the governing board of the National Social Science Association and a state liaison for Mississippi for Project Vote Smart. His research interests include foreign and security policy, and the U.S. presidency. Dr. Lansford is the author, coauthor, editor or coeditor of more than 40 books, and the author of more than one hundred essays, book chapters, encyclopedic entries, and reviews. Recent sole-authored books include: *A Bitter Harvest: U.S. Foreign Policy and Afghanistan* (2003), the *Historical Dictionary of U.S. Diplomacy Since the Cold War* (2007) and *9/11 and the Wars in Afghanistan and Iraq: A Chronology and Reference Guide* (2011). His more recent edited collections include: *America's War on Terror* (2003; second edition 2009), *Judging Bush* (2009), and *The Obama Presidency: A Preliminary Assessment* (2012). Dr. Lansford has served as the editor of the annual *Political Handbook of the World* since 2012.

PHOTO CREDITS